TRADITIONAL LOGIC
Introduction to Formal Logic

━━━ **BOOK I** ━━━

Answer Key

By Martin Cothran

CLASSICAL TRIVIUM CORE SERIES

TRADITIONAL LOGIC: BOOK I ANSWER KEY
Introduction to Formal Logic
© 2000 by Martin Cothran
ISBN: 978-1-930953-11-6

www.MemoriaPress.com

Table of Contents

QUIZZES & FINAL EXAM KEY

INTRODUCTION

_____ Exercises for Day 1

1. Logic is the science of right thinking.
2. Aristotle
3. Chrysippus
4. Gottfreid Wilhelm Leibniz
5. John Stuart Mill
6. Gottlob Frege, Alfred North Whitehead and Bertrand Russell
7. One is called _formal_ or "minor" logic, the other _material_ or "major" logic.
8. Formal logic is interested in the form or structure of reasoning.
9. Material logic is concerned with the content of argumentation. It deals with the truth of the terms and the propositions in an argument.
10. F (The purpose of formal logic is to lead us from one truth to another.)
    F (Formal logic is useful only if we already have truths to use logic with.)
    T
    T
    F (Statements can only be true or false.)
    F (Arguments can only be valid or invalid.)
    T
    T

_____ Exercises for Day 2

11. Truth is correspondence to reality.
12. We say an argument is valid when its conclusion follows logically from its premises.
13. The term _soundness_ is used to indicate that all the premises in an argument are true **and** that the argument is valid.
14. T
    F (A sound argument must both be valid and have true premises.)
    T
    F (A valid argument need not be sound, since an argument can be valid but have false premises, disallowing it from being sound.)
    T
    F (An argument must contain two premises in traditional logic.)
15.   All men are mortal   premise
           Socrates is a man   premise
           Therefore, Socrates is mortal   conclusion

16. Simple apprehension, judgment, and deductive inference.

_____ Exercises for Day 3

17. Mental act; verbal expression.
18. Simple apprehension.
19. Term.
20. We form in our minds a concept of something.
21. Book. (_Term_ would also be acceptable.)
22. Men; mortal; and Socrates.
23. A concept.
24. Judgment.
25. Proposition.
26. We perform a judgment any time we think in our minds that something is something else (which we call affirmation), and also when we think that something is _not_ something else (which we call denial).
27. Proposition.

Array

28. "All men are mortal"; "Socrates is a man"; and "Socrates is mortal." (You do not have to include the word 'therefore' in the last proposition.)
29. A judgment.

_____ **Exercises for Day 4**

30. Deductive inference.
31. Syllogism.
32. A deductive inference occurs when we make the logical connections in our minds between the terms in the argument in a way that shows us that the conclusion either follows or does not follow from the premises. (or something similar)
33. Syllogism.

34.

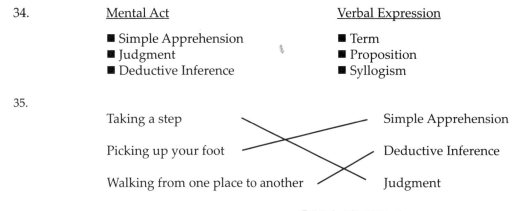

Mental Act	Verbal Expression
■ Simple Apprehension	■ Term
■ Judgment	■ Proposition
■ Deductive Inference	■ Syllogism

35.

Taking a step —————— Simple Apprehension

Picking up your foot —————— Deductive Inference

Walking from one place to another —————— Judgment

CHAPTER 1

_____ **Exercises for Day 1**

1. First, we perceive something with our senses; second, we form an of image of it in our mind; and, thirdly, we conceive its meaning.
2. The third: we conceive its meaning.
3. The first and second: perceiving something with our senses and forming an image of it in our minds.
4. The first: the perception of something with our senses.
5. Because the sense perception occurs in our minds, while the chair exists outside of our minds.
6. Sense perception is the act of seeing or hearing or smelling or tasting or touching.

_____ **Exercises for Day 2**

7. We form a mental image.
8. A mental image.
9. Because, while the sense perception lasts only as long as we are looking at the chair, the mental image can be present even when we are not perceiving the chair through our senses.
10. A mental image is the image of an object formed in the mind as a result of a sense perception of that object.
11. Simple apprehension.
12. Different.
13. Because, while a mental image is representative of something tangible and material (for example, it has shape and color), simple apprehension is the grasp of something intangible and immaterial.
14. *Simple apprehension* is an act by which the mind grasps the concept or general meaning of an object without affirming or denying anything about it.
15. Concept.

_____ **Exercises for Day 3**

16. We grasp the essence (or meaning) of the thing.
17. When we think of the concept *man*, we may have some kind of image in our mind, such as an actual man, tall, with blond hair, blue eyes and light skin. But when someone else thinks of the concept *man*, he may have a completely different image in his mind. He may think of an actual man who is short, with dark hair, brown eyes and dark skin. Although the mental images we have when we think of the concept *man* are completely different, that doesn't mean that we do not both understand the same concept *man*. We may have exactly the same understanding of what *man* is, yet have completely different mental images that we associate with it. (or something similar)
18. (This answer should be similar to the one in 17, only using another concept than *man*.)
19. The process by which a simple apprehension is derived from a sense perception or mental image is called *abstraction*.

_____ **Exercises for Day 4**

20. If you affirm or deny anything about a concept, you are going beyond simple apprehension and engaging in judgment.
21. F (Only the act of the mind grasping the essence or nature of a thing is the act itself.)
    T
    F (The chair exists outside the mind and the sense perception inside the mind.)
    T
    T
    T
    F (The idea of a chair in your mind need not be accompanied by the sense perception or the mental image.)
    F (While the simple apprehension is an act by which the mind grasps the concept or general meaning of an object, it does not affirm or deny anything about it. If it did, it would be a judgment, not a simple apprehension.)
    T
    F (Only sense perceptions and mental images can have shape and color.)
    T
    F (Mental images of the same essence can differ.)
    T
    T

_____ **Review Exercises**

22. Logic is the science of right thinking.
23. Correspondence to reality.
24. Simple apprehension; judgment; deductive inference.
25.
Mental Act	Verbal Expression
■ Simple Apprehension	■ Term
■ Judgment	■ Proposition
■ Deductive Inference	■ Syllogism

CHAPTER 2

_____ **Exercises for Day 1**

1. The properties of *simple apprehension*.
2. The two properties of simple apprehension are *comprehension* and *extension*.
3. Complex.
4. (Relatively) simple.
5. A featherless biped.
6. Yes.
7. It doesn't tell us many things about human beings that make up his nature or essence.
8. *Comprehension* can be defined as the completely articulated sum of the intelligible aspects, or elements (or notes) represented by a concept.
9. *Sentient*: having senses, such as sight, hearing, etc.; *material*: having a body, rather than being purely spiritual; *substance*: being something rather than nothing.

_____ **Exercises for Day 2**

10. Notes.
11. Four.
12. A sentient, living, material substance.
13. Five.
14. A rational, sentient, living, material substance.
15. The Porphyrian Tree.
16. It gives us a convenient way to break down a complex concept into the simple concepts out of which it is made.
17. Is it material substance or nonmaterial (or spiritual) substance? A chair is, of course, a material substance; in other words, it has *body* (the next level of the Porphyrian Tree). Now we know, then, that a chair is *material substance*. But what kind of material substance? Is it living material substance or nonliving material substance? A chair (let's say it is a metal chair instead of a wooden one) is a nonliving material substance, since metal cannot be said to be living. That is about as much as we can say about it. A chair, therefore, is a *nonliving material substance*.
18. Is an animal a material substance or nonmaterial (or spiritual) substance? An animal is, of course, a material substance; in other words, it has *body*. An animal, therefore, is a *material substance*. But what kind of material substance? Is it living material substance or nonliving material substance? An animal is a *living material substance*. Is it a sentient or non-sentient? It is *sentient*. So far, then, we know it is a *sentient, living, material substance*. Is it anything more? Is it *rational*? No. It is not. Therefore, we have said all we can say about it. An animal, then, is a *non-rational, sentient, living, material substance*.
19. Is a man a material substance or nonmaterial (or spiritual) substance? A man is, of course, a *material substance*; in other words, he has *body*. A man, therefore, is a *material substance*. But what kind of material substance? Is he living material substance or nonliving material substance? A man is a *living material substance*. Is he a sentient or non-sentient? He is sentient. So far, then, we know he is a *sentient, living, material substance*. Is it anything more? Is he rational? Yes. He is. Therefore, we know that a man is a *rational, sentient, living, material substance*.

_____ **Exercises for Day 3**

20. The second of the two properties of simple apprehension we study in this chapter is the property of *extension*.
21. All the men who have ever lived, who are now living and who will live in the future.
22. All the animals who have ever lived, who are now living and who will live in the future.
23. Comprehension tells us what the essence of a thing is; extension tells us the things to which that essence applies.
24. Man, because the concept *man* has more notes than the concept *animal*.
25. Animal, because there are, have been and will be more of them.
26. Body.
27. Man.
28. less; less.

_____ **Exercises for Day 4**

29. F (They are *comprehension* and *extention*, not *concept* and *extension*.)
    T
    F (Aristotle said this, not Porphry.)
    T (The student might say this is false, thinking that it is substance, rather than being *sentient* that determines whether it is something rather than nothing; however, if something is sentient, then it must be a substance [there are no things that are sentient that are not substance] and therefore it must be something rather than nothing.)
    F (The concept *man* has 5 notes.)
    T
    F (There are fewer men who have ever lived, are living, and ever will live than there are things that have material substance that ever were, are, or will be.)
    T
    T
30. An automobile is a non-living material substance.
31. All the automobiles that have ever been made, that are now being made, and that ever will be made.
32. (The answer to this question should be similar to the answers to Questions 30 and 31.)

_____ **Review Exercises**

33. T
    F (While the simple apprehension is an act by which the mind grasps the concept or general meaning of an object, it does not affirm or deny anything about it. If it did, it would be a judgment, not a simple apprehension.)
    T
    T
    T

34.
Mental Act	Verbal Expression
■ Simple Apprehension	■ Term
■ Judgment	■ Proposition
■ Deductive Inference	■ Syllogism

CHAPTER 3

_____ **Exercises for Day 1**

1. Terms.
2. A term is a word or group of words which verbally expresses a concept.
3. Signification and supposition.
4. Terms can be divided according to their signification in three ways. There are _univocal terms_, _equivocal terms_ and _analogous terms_.

_____ **Exercises for Day 2**

5. Univocal terms are terms that have exactly the same meaning no matter when or how they are used.
6. photosynthesis, anthropology, the second law of thermodynamics, tablesaw, phillips head screwdriver and drill bit.
7. Scientific or manufacturing terms.
8. "One voice."
9. (Make sure answers to this question are terms that have exactly the same meaning no matter when or how they are used.)
10. Equivocal terms, are terms that, although spelled and pronounced exactly alike, have entirely different and unrelated meanings.
11. Pitcher, plane, and jar.
12. Puns.
13. "Equal voice."
14. (Make sure answers to this question are terms that, although spelled and pronounced exactly alike, have entirely different and unrelated meanings.)
15. Analogous terms are terms that are applied to different things, but have related meanings.
16. Window, wheel, and wooden.
17. In poetry and literature.
18. (Make sure answers to this question are terms that are applied to different things, but have related meanings.)
19. Terms must be defined accurately in order to use proper logic.

_____ **Exercises for Day 3**

20. According to their verbal, mental or real existence.
21. Material supposition occurs when a term refers to something as it exists verbally.
22. "_Man_ is a three-letter word."
23. (Make sure the term used in material supposition in this answer uses the term in reference to something as it exists verbally, as in "_man_ is a three-letter word," "_man_ is a phonetic word," etc.)
24. Logical supposition occurs when a term refers to something as it exists logically.
25. "Man has five notes."
26. (Make sure the term used in logical supposition in this answer uses the term in reference to something as it exists logically, as in "_man_ has three notes," "the concept _man_ has less extension than _body_," etc.)
27. Real supposition occurs when a term refers to something as it exists in the real world.
28. "Man was created by God."
29. (Make sure the term used in real supposition in this answer uses the term in reference to something as it exists in the real world, as in "Man was created by God," "Some men are brave," etc.)

_____ **Exercises for Day 4: Review of Introduction-Chapter 3**

30.   <u>Mental Act</u>   <u>Verbal Expression</u>
        ■ Simple Apprehension   ■ Term
        ■ Judgment   ■ Proposition
        ■ Deductive Inference   ■ Syllogism

31. The definition of simple apprehension
32. The properties of simple apprehension (comprehension and extension).
33. The properties of terms (signification and supposition).

34. Equivocal terms 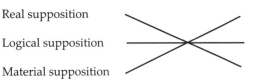 terms that have exactly the same meaning no matter when or how they are used

Univocal terms   terms that, although spelled and pronounced exactly alike, have entirely different and unrelated meanings

Analogous terms   terms that are applied to different things but have related meanings

35. Real supposition   occurs when a term refers to something as it exists verbally

Logical supposition   occurs when a term refers to something as it exists logically

Material supposition   occurs when a term refers to something as it exists in the real world

36. F (They are the properties of _simple apprehension_.)
     T
     F (It is an example of a _univocal term_.)
     T
     F (They have entirely different and unrelated meanings, even though they are spelled or pronounced exactly the same way)
     F (Analogous terms are applied to different terms but have related meanings.)
     T
     F (_Window_ is an analogous term.)
     T
     F (scientific terms are primarily univocal terms)
     F (This is how terms are divided up according to their _supposition_, not their _signification_.)
     F (Material supposition occurs when a term refers to something as it exists _verbally_.)
     F (See explanation of previous answer.)
     T
     T
     T

CHAPTER 4

_____ **Exercises for Day 1**

1. Judgment.
2. Term.
3. Proposition.
4. Second.
5. Judgment can be defined as the act by which the intellect unites by affirming, or separates by denying.
6. Two concepts.
7. The two concepts _man_ and _animal_.
8. The two concepts _man_ and _God_.
9. The subject and the predicate.
10. The subject is that about which we are saying something; it is the concept about which we are affirming or denying something.
11. The predicate is what it is we are saying about the subject; it is what we are affirming or denying about it.
12. _Man_ is the subject and _animal_ is the predicate.
13. The subject is _man_ and the predicate is _God_.
14. That he is an animal (biologically).
15. That he is not God.

_____ **Exercises for Day 2**

16. A sentence or statement which expresses truth or falsity.
17. Questions, commands, exclamations, and greetings.
18.

	Proposition	Not a proposition
Peter is a man.	☑	☐
Just do it.	☐	☑
Where in the world is Carmen San Diego?	☐	☑
Peter is not a man.	☑	☐
There were three thousand purple ducks found on Mars.	☑	☐
Barney (the purple dinosaur) is a man.	☑	☐
Oh wow.	☐	☑
Hello!	☐	☑
All dogs go to heaven.	☑	☐
No purple dinosaurs go to heaven.	☑	☐
Who is President of the United States?	☐	☑
Barney is President of the United States.	☑	☐
The postman never rings twice.	☑	☐
How are you today?	☐	☑
That's a fine duck you have there.	☑	☐
How many ducks do you have?	☐	☑
Don't feed the animals.	☐	☑
Peter is not a duck.	☑	☐

19. (Make sure that none of the sentences given in answer to this question are questions, commands, exclamations or greetings.)
20. (Make sure that the sentences given in answer to this question are not sentences that express truth or falsity.)

_____ **Exercises for Day 3**

21. The subject, the predicate and the copula.
22. 'S' stands for subject; 'P' stands for predicate; 'c' stands for copula.
23. The subject-term is the verbal expression of the subject of a judgment.
24. The predicate-term is the verbal expression of the predicate of a judgment.
25. A copula is a form of the _to be_ verb (e.g., _is, are_, etc.) that connects the subject and the predicate.
26. A subject-term can be made up of many words.
27. A predicate-term can be made up of many words.
28. Peter is a man.   S: "Peter"; P: "a man"; c: "is"
    Two and two are four.   S: "Two and two"; P: "four"; c: "are"
    I am the vine.   S: "I"; P: "the vine"; c: "am"
    You are the branches.   S: "You"; P: "the branches"; c: "are"
    I am the Son of God.   S: "I"; P: "the Son of God"; c: "am"
    My kingdom is not of this world (ignore "not" for purposes of this exercise).
                                  S: "My kingdom"; P: "not of this world"; c: "is"

_____ **Exercises for Day 4**

29. It is in logical form if the subject, predicate and copula are easily distinguishable.
30. By reworking the predicate-copula portion of the sentence to make it more explicit.
31.

	Logical form	Not logical form
Peter is a man.	☑	☐
My nose is big.	☑	☐
Peter is big.	☑	☐
I am the way and the truth and the life.	☑	☐
He that seeth me seeth Him that sent me.	☐	☑
Man thinks.	☐	☑
Roses are red.	☑	☐
Three is a crowd.	☐	☑
I like it.	☐	☑
Home is where the heart is.	☑	☐

32. "He that seeth me is a person (is someone, etc.) who seeth Him that sent me."
    "Man is a being (creature, etc.) who thinks."
    "Three (people) is a crowd."
    "I am a person who likes it."
33. T
    F (because a judgment could also separate two concepts by denying)
    F (Deductive inference is the third part of the study of logic.)
    F (The subject and the predicate are united by the copula.)
    F (The subject of the sentence is *man*.)
    F (The subject is *man*.)
    T
    F (It is a command, not a proposition.)
    T
    T
    F (It can have one or more words.)

CHAPTER 5

_____ Exercises for Day 1

1. The classification of propositions.
2. "All S is P"; "Some S is P"; "No S is P"; and "Some S is not P"
3. A, I, E, and O
4. "A" stands for the first vowel in the Latin word *affirmo*.
5. "I" stands for the second vowel in the Latin word *affirmo*.
6. "E" stands for the first vowel in the Latin word *nego*.
7. "O" stands for the second vowel in the Latin word *nego*.
8.
All men are mortal: A	No girls are pretty: E
Some men are not mortal: O	Some cars are not fast: O
No boys are rude: E	All boys are rude: A
All cars are fast: A	Some girls are not pretty: O
Some men are mortal: I	All girls are pretty: A
Some boys are rude: I	Some cars are fast: I
No men are mortal: E	No cars are fast: E
Some boys are not rude: O	Some girls are pretty: I
9. The quantifier.
10. "All," "Some," "No," and "Some … not"
11. All men are mortal: "All"
    Some men are mortal: "Some"
    No men are mortal: "No"
    Some men are not mortal: "Some … not"
12.
"All"	"No"
"Some …. not"	"Some … not"
"No"	"All"
"All"	"Some … not"
"Some"	"All"
"Some"	"Some"
"No"	"No"
"Some … not"	"Some"
13. Quality and Quantity.

_____ Exercises for Day 2

14. The quality of a proposition has to do with whether it is affirmative or negative.
15. Whether it is affirmative or negative.
16. We mean that something is affirmed about the subject of the sentence.
17. We mean that something is denied about the subject of the sentence.
18. All S is P: _affirmative_
    Some S is P: _affirmative_
    No S is P: _negative_
    Some S is not P: _negative_
19. All men are mortal: _affirmative_   No girls are pretty: _negative_
    Some men are not mortal: _negative_   Some cars are fast: _affirmative_
    No boys are rude: _negative_   All boys are rude: _affirmative_
    All cars are fast: _affirmative_   Some girls are not pretty: _negative_
    Some men are mortal: _affirmative_   All girls are pretty: _affirmative_
    Some boys are rude: _affirmative_   Some cars are fast: _affirmative_
    No men are mortal: _negative_   No cars are fast: _negative_
    Some boys are not rude: _negative_   Some girls are pretty: _affirmative_
20. (Make sure the answers to this question include the quantifiers _All_ or _some_.)
21. (Make sure the answers to this question include the quantifiers _No_ or _some ... not_.)

_____ Exercises for Day 3

22. The quantity of a proposition has to do with whether it is universal or particular.
23. We are asking whether it is universal or particular.
24. We mean that the proposition says something about all the members of the class referred to by the subject of the proposition.
25. We mean that the proposition says something about only some of the members of the class referred to by the subject of the proposition.
26. All S is P: _universal_
    Some S is P: _particular_
    No S is P: _universal_
    Some S is not P: _particular_
27. All men are mortal: _universal_   No girls are pretty: _universal_
    Some men are not mortal: _particular_   Some cars are fast: _particular_
    No boys are rude: _universal_   All boys are rude: _universal_
    All cars are fast: _universal_   Some girls are not pretty: _particular_
    Some men are mortal: _particular_   All girls are pretty: _universal_
    Some boys are rude: _particular_   Some cars are fast: _particular_
    No men are mortal: _universal_   No cars are fast: _universal_
    Some boys are not rude: _particular_   Some girls are pretty: _particular_
28. (The propositions given in answer to this question should include the quantifiers _All_ or _No_.)
29. (The propositions given in answer to this question should include the quantifiers _Some_ or _Some ... not_.)

_____ Exercises for Day 4

30. The general rule for statements that do not contain a quantifier is that "all" is intended, unless "some" is clearly indicated.
31. Statements in which the subject-term is the name of a certain individual are universal, since they refer to all the members of the class referred to by the name, even though that class happens to be made up of only one person.
32. Caesar is a great general: _universal_
    Mary is the mother of Jesus: _universal_
    The soldiers are tired: _universal_ (since it seems to indicate all the soldiers)
    Jesus is the Son of God: _universal_
    Christians pray: _universal_ (Although the statement seems to indicate all Christians, you could argue that all Christians do not in fact pray. But the implication appears to be _universal_.)
    Albert Einstein was a genius: _universal_
    Romans are cruel: _universal_ (the same qualification here as we discussed in "Christians pray" above)

33. All kings are good: *affirmative, universal*
No truth is simple: *negative, universal*
Some generals are great: *affirmative, particular*
Some Gauls are not brave: *negative, particular*
All Romans are brave: *affirmative, universal*
Some wars are not cruel: *negative, particular*
All Christians are brothers: *affirmative, universal*
No wars are peaceful: *negative, universal*

Some towns are well-fortified: *affirmative, particular*
All truth is God's truth: *affirmative, universal*
Some towns are not fortified: *negative, particular*
Some victories are not glorious: *negative, particular*
No tribes are safe: *negative, universal*
All leaders are slaughtered: *affirmative, universal*
Some wars are fierce: *affirmative, particular*
No kings are good: *negative, universal*

34.

		Quality	
		Affirmative	Negative
Quantity	Universal	A	E
	Particular	I	O

_____ Review Exercises for Day 4

35. By reworking the predicate-copula portion of the sentence.
36. T
F (Deductive inference is the third part of the study of logic.)
F (The subject and the predicate are united by the copula.)
F (It is a command, not a proposition.)
T
F (It can have one or more words.)

CHAPTER 6

_____ Exercises for Day 1

1.   Opposition and equivalence.
2.   We mean the relationship which we observe in things we call *opposite*.
3.   We affirm or deny the same predicate of the same subject.
4.   They can be *contradictory* to one another, *contrary*, *subcontrary*, or *subalternate*.
5.   Contradictory statements are statements that differ in both quality and quantity.
6.   The A statement is affirmative and universal.
7.   The O statement is negative and particular
8.   Yes. The A statement contradicts the O statement because they differ in both quality (the A statement is affirmative, while the O statement is negative) and quantity (the A statement is universal, while the O statement is particular.)
9.   The E statement and the I statement are contradictory to one another, since they differ in both quality and quantity.
10. The 3rd, 4th, 11th, and 12th pairs of statements are contradictory to one another.

_____ Exercises for Day 2

11. Contradictories cannot at the same time be true nor at the same time false.
12. No.
13. No.
14. No.
15. No.
16. A and O statements and E and I statements.
17. The 2nd, 3rd, 10th, and 11th pairs of statements are contradictory.
18. Because they must differ in both quality and quantity, but A and E only differ in quality.

_____ **Exercises for Day 3**

19. Two statements are contrary to one another if they are both universals but differ in quality.
20. The A statement is affirmative and universal.
21. The E statement is negative and universal.
22. Yes. The A statement is contrary to the E statement because they are both universals which differ in quality.
23. There is no other pair of statements which are contrary to one another.
24. The 2nd, 5th, 10th, and 13th pairs of statements are contrary to one another.
25. Contraries cannot at the same time both be true, but can at the same time both be false.
26. The A and E statements.
27. The 1st, 4th, 9th, and 12th pairs of statements are contrary to one another.
28. In order for two statements to be contraries, they must both be universals and differ in quality. Although the A and O statements do differ in quality (the A statement is affirmative and the O statement is negative), they are not both universals. Therefore, they cannot be contraries.
29. Although they differ in quality, they are not both universal.

_____ **Exercises for Day 4**

30.

| | | Quality | |
		Affirmative	Negative
Quantity	Universal	A	E
	Particular	I	O

31. See Figure 6-2.
32. (The statements given in answer to this question should differ in both quality and quantity.)
33. (The statements given in answers to this question should both be universal but differ in quality.)
34. F (They must also differ with each other in quantity.)
    F (Its _quantity_ is universal, but its _quality_ is affirmative.)
    T
    T
    F (They cannot both be true, although they can both be false.)
    T
    T
    F ("Just do it" is not a proposition at all.)
    T
    F (Contrary statements cannot both be true, but can both be false.)

_____ **Review Exercises for Day 4**

35. The verbal expression of a judgment is a proposition.
36. It is in logical form if the subject, predicate and copula are easily distinguishable.
37. Universal, because they refer to all members of the class indicated by the name, even though the name indicates only one person.

CHAPTER 7

_____ **Exercises for Day 1**

1. They can be _contradictory_ to one another, _contrary_, _subcontrary_, and _subalternate_.
2. Subcontrariness and subalternation.
3. Two statements are subcontrary if they are both particular statements that differ in quality.
4. The I statement is affirmative and particular.
5. The O statement is negative and particular.
6. Yes. I and O statements are subcontrary to one another because they are both particular and differ in quality.
7. No other two statements are subcontrary to one another.
8. Only the 7th and 8th pairs of statements are subcontrary to one another.

_____ **Exercises for Day 2**

9. Subcontraries may at the same time be true, but cannot at the same time be false.
10. Yes.
11. No.
12. I and O statements.
13. The 6th and 7th pairs of statements.
14. The A and E statements are not subcontrary because, although they differ in quality, they are not both particular.

_____ **Exercises for Day 3**

15. Two statements are subalternate if they have the same quality, but differ in quantity.
16. The A statement is affirmative and universal.
17. The I statement is affirmative and particular.
18. Yes, because they have the same quality, but differ in quantity.
19. Yes: E and O statements.
20. The 1st, 6th, 9th, and 14th pairs of statements are subalternate.
21. Subalterns may both be true or both be false. If the particular is false, the universal is false; if the universal is true, then the particular is true; otherwise, their status is indeterminate.
22. A and I statements and E and O statements.
23. Yes.
24. Yes.
25. Yes.
26. Yes.
27. The 5th, 8th, 13th, and 14th pairs of statements are subalternate.
28. The A and E statements are not subalternate because they are not the same in quality nor do they differ in quantity.
29. The I and O statements are not subalternate because they are not the same in quality nor do they differ in quantity.

_____ **Exercises for Day 4**

30.

		Quality	
		Affirmative	Negative
Quantity	Universal	A	E
	Particular	I	O

31. See Figure 7-2.
32. (The pairs statements given in answer to this question must both be particular but differ in quality.)
33. (The pairs of statements given in answer to this question should be the same in quality but differ in quantity.)
34. T
    F (It is the _quantity_, not the _quality_ of the statement that is universal.)
    T
    F (They only differ in _quantity_.)
    T
    T
    T
    F (The statement "Just do it" isn't even a proposition.)
    T
    F (Subalternate statements can both be false.)

_____ **Review Exercises for Day 4**

35. Contradictories cannot at the same time be true nor at the same time false.
36. Contraries cannot at the same time both be true, but can at the same time be false.
37. No.
38. No.

39. No.
40. No.
41. No.
42. Yes.

CHAPTER 8

_____ **Exercises for Day 1**

1. The distribution of terms.
2. Distribution is the status of a term in regard to extension.
3. The subject of a statement is the term about which the statement is saying something.
4. *Men* is the subject.
5. *Mortal* is the predicate.
6. We mean that the term refers to all the members of the class of things denoted by the term.
7. Distributed.
8. Undistributed.

_____ **Exercises for Day 2**

9. The subject-term is distributed in statements whose quantity is universal and undistributed in statements whose quantity is particular.
10. Because the quantifier tells us all we need to know.
11. Distributed.
12. Distributed.
13. Undistributed.
14. Undistributed.
15. Quantifier.
16.

Type of sentence	Subject-Term
A	Distributed
I	Undistributed
E	Distributed
O	Undistributed

17. Tell whether the subjects in the following statements are distributed or undistributed.

Distributed	Distributed
Distributed	Distributed
Undistributed	Undistributed
Undistributed	Undistributed
Distributed	Distributed
Distributed	Distributed

_____ **Exercises for Day 3**

18. In affirmative propositions the predicate-term is always taken particularly (and therefore undistributed) and in negative propositions the predicate is always taken universally (and therefore distributed).
19. Undistributed.
20. Distributed.
21. Undistributed.
22. Distributed.
23.   24.   25.   26.

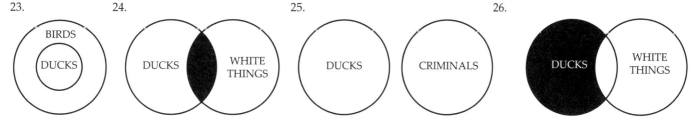

27.
DIAGRAM OF THE DISTRIBUTION OF TERMS IN A, I, E, AND O STATEMENTS

Type of sentence	Subject-Term	Predicate-Term
A	Distributed	Undistributed
I	Undistributed	Undistributed
E	Distributed	Distributed
O	Undistributed	Distributed

28. No cars are fast. S: **D** UnD P: **D** UnD
Some omelettes are tasty. S: D **UnD** P: D **UnD**
Some tomatoes are not red. S: D **UnD** P: **D** UnD
Michael Jordan is a good basketball player. S: **D** UnD P: D **UnD**
No guns are loud. S: **D** UnD P: **D** UnD
Some rocks are crystals. S: D **UnD** P: D **UnD**
Some men are sinners. S: D **UnD** P: D **UnD**
No men are saved. S: **D** UnD P: **D** UnD
All wars are bloody. S: **D** UnD P: D **UnD**
Some soldiers are not brave. S: D **UnD** P: **D** UnD
Some animals are amphibians. S: D **UnD** P: D **UnD**
No houses are well-built. S: **D** UnD P: **D** UnD
All storms are violent. S: **D** UnD P: D **UnD**
All machines are loud. S: **D** UnD P: D **UnD**

_____ Exercises for Day 4

29. Although there are some vicious things that are not dogs, there are no carpenters who are not men.
30. Although there are some blind things that are not men, there are no carpenters who are not men.

31.
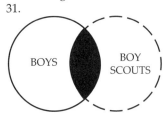

32.
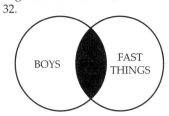

33.
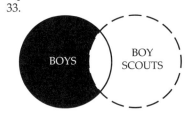

34.
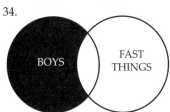

35. All dogs are mammals.
36. Some men are violent.
37. No dogs are immortal.
38. Some dogs are not long-haired.
39. T
   F (The subject term is distributed in universal statements.)
   T
   F (The subject term is distributed in universal statements. E statements are universal.)
   F (No: I statements are affirmative, and the subject term is not distributed.)
   T

_____ **Review Exercises for Day 4**

40.

| | | Quality | |
		Affirmative	Negative
Quantity	Universal	A	E
	Particular	I	O

41. See Figure 7-2.
42. T
F (The statement "Just do it" is not even a proposition.)
T
F (They can be false at the same time.)

CHAPTER 9

_____ **Exercises for Day 1**

1. The different ways in which propositions are equivalent.
2. We use the phrase _logically equivalent_.
3. Obversion, conversion, and contraposition.
4. 1) Change the quality of the sentence; 2) Negate the predicate.
5. If the statement is affirmative, then you make it negative; if it is negative, you make affirmative.
6. No logic problems are difficult.
   All logic problems are difficult.
   Some logic problems are not difficult.
   Some logic problems are difficult.
   Some men are not white.
   No men are white.
   Some men are white.
   All men are white.
7. Simply place a "_not_" in front of it.
8. All logic problems are _not_ difficult.
   No logic problems are _not_ difficult.
   Some logic problems are _not_ difficult.
   Some logic problems are _not_ not difficult. (We will talk about how to deal with double negatives later.)
   Some men are _not_ white.
   All men are _not_ white.
   Some men are _not_ not white.
   No men are _not_ white.
9. It can be used with all four categorical statements.
10. You get a double-negation.
11. Because you have to negate a predicate which already has a _not_ in it.
12. First, you can simply have two _nots_ in the statement, right next to each other. Second, you can make the _not_ directly in front of the predicate a _non_. Third, you can incorporate the second negation in the predicate word itself by placing an _im, un, in,_ or _ir_ at the beginning of the word you are using in the predicate. Finally, you can apply the rule of double negation.
13. There are some words which, when _im, un, in,_ or _ir_ are placed at the beginning of the word, are not the actual negation of the original word.
14. No. The negation of the thing to which the predicate refers may not be either large or small, but somewhere in between.
15. No logic problems are not difficult.
    All logic problems are not difficult.
    Some logic problems are not non-difficult.
    Some logic problems are not difficult.
    Some men are not non-white.
    No men are non-white.
    Some men are not white.
    All men are non-white.

_____ **Exercises for Day 2**

16. The rule of double negation says that a term which is not negated is equivalent to a term that is negated twice and vice-versa.
17. mortal   white

    not non-immortal   not not non-white

    not immortal   not non-white

    immortal   white

    not illogical   animal

    not non-illogical   not not non-animal

    illogical   not non-animal

    logical   non-animal
18. Two.
19. The one you started with.
20. We should apply it when it makes the statement sound less awkward and not apply it when it doesn't.
21. You interchange the subject and the predicate.
22. The E and the I statements can be converted.
23. N/A

    No difficult things are logic problems.

    Some difficult things are logic problems.

    N/A

    Some white things are men.

    N/A

    N/A

    No white things are men.
24. It can be partially converted into an I statement. Partial conversion of the A statement is done by interchanging the subject and predicate and changing the statement from universal to particular.
25. Some oxygen-breathing things are mammals.

    Some brave people are Americans.

    Some smelly things are pigs.

    Some fast things are horses.

    Some loud things are babies.

    Some quiet things are oysters.

    Some angry things are lobsters.

    Some irrational things are geraniums.

_____ **Exercises for Day 3**

26. Obvert the statement, convert it, and obvert it again.
27. The A and O statements.
28. All men are mortal.   Step 1: No men are immortal.

                             Step 2: No immortal things are men.

                             Step 3: All immortal things are not men.

    All men are animals.   Step 1: No men are not animals.

                             Step 2: No non-animals are men.

                             Step 3: All non-animals are not men.

    All pigs are smelly.   Step 1: No pigs are not smelly.

                             Step 2: No non-smelly things are pigs.

                             Step 3: All non-smelly things are not pigs.

    All oysters are quiet.   Step 1: No oysters are not quiet.

                             Step 2: No non-quiet things are oysters.

                             Step 3: All non-quiet things are not oysters.

    All lobsters are angry.   Step 1: No lobsters are not angry.

                             Step 2: No non-angry things are lobsters.

                             Step 3: All non-angry things are not lobsters.

29. All non-difficult things are not logic problems.
N/A
N/A
Some things that are not difficult are logic problems.
N/A
All non-white things are not men.
Some non-white things are men.
N/A

30. N/A
N/A
Some non-red things are tomatoes.
All people who are not good basketball
    players are not Michael Jordan.
N/A
N/A
N/A

    N/A
    All non-bloody events are not wars.
    Some non-brave people are soldiers.
    N/A

    N/A
    All non-violent things are not storms.
    All non-loud things are not machines.

_____ Exercises for Day 4

31. Sentences given in answer to this question should follow the following pattern:

All S is P	------------------>	No S is not P
No S is P	------------------>	All S is not P
Some S is P	-------------->	Some S is not non-P
Some S is not P	--------->	Some S is not P

32. Sentences given in answer to this question should follow the following pattern:

No S is P	------------>	No P is S
Some S is P	-------->	Some P is S

33. Sentences given in answer to this question should follow the following pattern:

All S is P	------------------>	All non-P is non-S
Some S is not P	--------->	Some non-P is S

34. O
C
C
CP
CP
C
O
C
O
CP
CP
O
O
CP

35. F (The three ways are obversion, conversion, and contraposition.)
T
T
F
F (It must obverted, converted, and then obverted again.)
F (They are obverse, not contrapositive.)
T

_____ Review Exercises for Day 4

36. _Judgment_ can be defined as the act by which the intellect unites by affirming, or separates by denying.
37. A _proposition_ is a sentence or statement which expresses truth or falsity.
38. The four elements of a proposition are the _subject, predicate, copula,_ and _quantifier_.
39. We say a statement is in proper logical form when the elements of a logical proposition are clearly distinguished.
40. A: All S is P; I: Some S is P; E: No S is P; and O: Some S is not P.

41. Quality and quantity.
42.

		Quality	
		Affirmative	Negative
Quantity	Universal	A	E
	Particular	I	O

43. Two statements are contradictory if they differ in both quality and quantity.
44. Two statements are contrary if they are both universal but differ in quality.
45. Two statements are subcontrary if they are both particular statements that differ in quality.
46. Two statements are subalternate if they have the same quality, but differ in quantity.
47. See Figure 7-2.
48. Distribution is the status of a term in regard to its extension.

49.
DIAGRAM OF THE DISTRIBUTION OF
TERMS IN A, E, I, AND O STATEMENTS

Type of sentence	Subject-Term	Predicate-Term
A	Distributed	Undistributed
I	Undistributed	Undistributed
E	Distributed	Distributed
O	Undistributed	Distributed

50.
Chapter	Topic
Ch. 4:	The definition of judgment and how a proposition (the verbal expression of a judgment) is constructed.
Ch. 5:	The four logical statements and their quality and quantity.
Chs. 6-7:	The ways in which propositions can be logically opposed to one another.
Ch. 8:	The distribution of terms.
Ch. 9:	The ways in which propositions can be logically equivalent.

CHAPTER 10

_____ Exercises for Day 1

1. Syllogism, which is the verbal expression of deductive inference.
2.

Mental Act	Verbal Expression
■ Simple Apprehension	■ Term
■ Judgment	■ Proposition
■ Deductive Inference	■ Syllogism

3. Reasoning is the act by which the mind acquires new knowledge by means of what it already knows.
4. The two kinds of reasoning are deductive and inductive.
5. Deductive.
6. First, we perceive the first premise as being true. Secondly, we perceive that the second premise is also true. The third step is an act of deductive inference. This third step takes place when we realize that, given the truth of the two premises, the conclusion must also be true.
7. The antecedent.
8. The consequent.
9. Because the mind stops or "concludes" at this step.
10. Deductive inference is the act by which the mind establishes a connection between the antecedent and the consequent.
11. A syllogism is a group of propositions in orderly sequence, one of which (the consequent) is said to be necessarily inferred from the others (the antecedent).

12. All men are mortal	Antecedent	N/A
Socrates is a man	Antecedent	
Therefore, Socrates is mortal	Consequent	
No men are gods	Antecedent	N/A
Socrates is a man	Antecedent	
Therefore, Socrates is not a god	Consequent	
All birds are able to fly	Antecedent	C1
The ostrich is a bird.	Antecedent	
Therefore, the ostrich is able to fly	Consequent	
All apostles are men	Antecedent	N/A
Peter is an apostle	Antecedent	
Therefore, Peter is a man	Consequent	
All fish can live out of water	Antecedent	C2
A dog is a fish	Antecedent	
Therefore, a dog can live out of water	Consequent	
All men are sinners	Antecedent	C1
My dog Spot is a man	Antecedent	
Therefore, my dog Spot is a sinner	Consequent	
No ducks are birds	Antecedent	C1
A Mallard is a duck	Antecedent	
Therefore, a mallard is not a bird	Consequent	
All reptiles can fly	Antecedent	C1
A horse is a reptile	Antecedent	
Therefore, a horse can fly	Consequent	

No beliefs that conflict with the Bible are true	Antecedent	N/A
The belief that the world is a product of chance conflicts with the Bible	Antecedent	
Therefore, the belief that the world is a product of chance is not true	Consequent	

13. If the antecedent is true, the consequent must also be true.
14. If the syllogism is valid and the consequent is false, then the antecedent (i.e., one or both of the two premises) must be false.
15. In a valid syllogism with a true consequent, the antecedent is not necessarily true.
16. See answers to Question 12.

_____ **Exercises for Day 2**

17. The major, minor, and middle terms.
18. Explain how to distinguish each of the following:
    Major term: it is the predicate of the conclusion.
    Minor term: it is the subject of the conclusion.
    Middle term: it is the term which is found in both of the premises but not in the conclusion.
19. The premise that contains the major term.
20. The premise that contains the minor term.
21.

All men are mortal	Major premise	Major term: 'mortal'
Socrates is a man	Minor premise	Minor term: 'Socrates'
Therefore, Socrates is mortal		Middle term: 'man'
All logic problems are difficult	Major premise	Major term: 'difficult thing'
This problem is a logic problem	Minor premise	Minor term: 'problem'
This problem is difficult		Middle term: 'logic problem'

All good basketball players can shoot well	Major premise	Major term: 'people who can shoot well'
Michael Jordan is a good basketball player	Minor premise	Minor term: 'Michael Jordan'
Therefore, Michael Jordan can shoot well		Middle term: 'good basketball player'

No men are gods	Major premise	Major term: 'god'
Socrates is a man	Minor premise	Minor term: 'Socrates'
Therefore, Socrates is not a god		Middle term: 'man'

All apostles are men	Major premise	Major term: 'man'
Peter is an apostle	Minor premise	Minor term: 'Peter'
Therefore, Peter is a man		Middle term: 'apostle'

No beliefs that conflict with the Bible are true
The belief that the world was created by chance conflicts with the Bible
Therefore, the belief that the world was created by chance is not true

	Major premise	Major term: 'true beliefs'
	Minor premise	Minor term: 'belief that the world was created by chance'
		Middle term: 'beliefs that conflict with the Bible'

_____ Exercises for Day 3

22. Two terms that are identical with a third term are identical to each other.
23. Two terms, one of which is identical with a third term and the other of which is nonidentical with that third term, are nonidentical to each other.
24. What is affirmed universally of a certain term is affirmed of every term that comes under that term.
25. What is denied universally of a certain term is denied of every term that comes under that term.
26.

PRI	DO
PRI	DO
PRI	DO
PRNI	DN
PRNI	DN
PRI	DO

_____ Exercises for Day 4

27.

All mammals^M breathe oxygen^P	Major premise
A horse^S is a mammal^M	Minor premise
Therefore, a horse^S breathes oxygen^P	

All Americans^M are brave^P	Major premise
George Washington^S is an American^M	Minor premise
Therefore, George Washington^S is brave^P	

All horses^M are fast^P	Major premise
Secretariat^S is a horse^M	Minor premise
Therefore, Secretariat^S is fast^P	

All wars^M are bloody^P	Major premise
The War of the Roses^S was a war^M	Minor premise
Therefore, the War of the Roses^S was bloody^P	

28. These syllogisms should be similar in structure to the first syllogism in Question 21.
29. F (It is the act of the mind by which we derive one truth from other truths we already know.)
   T
   F (It contains two premises.)
   T
   T
   T
   F (It is in both premises, but not the conclusion.)
   T

CHAPTER 11

———————— **Exercises for Day 1**

1. The first category of rules for the validity of syllogisms.
2. Terminological Rules:
   I.   There must be three and only three terms.
   II. The middle term must not occur in the conclusion.
   Quantitative Rules:
   III. If a term is not distributed in the premises, then it must not be distributed in the conclusion.
   IV. The middle term must be distributed at least once.
   Qualitative Rules:
   V.   No conclusion can follow from two negative premises.
   VI. If the two premises are affirmative, the conclusion must also be affirmative.
   VII. If either premise is negative, the conclusion must be negative.
3. All seven.
4. The first two, the terminological rules.
5. Because they have specifically to do with the terms in a syllogism.
6. The major, minor, and middle terms.
7. The major term is the predicate of the conclusion; the minor term is the subject of the conclusion; the middle term is the term that appears in both premises, but not in the conclusion.
8. The premise which contains the minor term.
9. The premise which contains the major term.
10. All plants^M are living things^P Major premise
    A daisy^S is a plant^M Minor premise
    Therefore, a daisy^S is a living thing^P

    All angels^M are created by God^P Major premise
    Gabriel^S is an angel^M Minor premise
    Gabriel^S is created by God^P

    All men^M are sinners^P Major premise
    I^S am a man^M Minor premise
    Therefore, I^S am a sinner^P

    No animal^M is rational^P Major premise
    My dog Spot^S is an animal^M Minor premise
    Therefore, my dog Spot^S is not rational^P

———————— **Exercises for Day 2**

11. There must be three and only three terms.
12. The Fallacy of Four Terms and the Fallacy of Equivocation.
13. The Fallacy of Four Terms is committed when there are four clearly distinguishable terms in a syllogism.
14. The Fallacy of Equivocation is committed when one of the three terms is used in argument in two different senses.
15. A term is an equivocal term when it can be used with two entirely different meanings.
16. All wildebeasts... FFT   All mice ... FE

    All animals ...   FFT   All kings ... FFT

    All accidents ... FE   All aliens ... FE

    All banks ...   FE   All roses ... FFT

_____ **Exercises for Day 3**

17. The syllogisms given in answer to this question should have three and only three distinguishable terms.
18. The middle term must not occur in the conclusion.

19&20.
Yes:	felines	No:	animals
No:	animals	Yes:	kings
No:	things that are life-threatening	No:	aliens
No:	things that contain water	Yes:	beautiful things

_____ **Exercises for Day 4**

21. Syllogisms given in answer to this question should have three and only three distinguishable terms and should not have the middle term in the conclusion.
22. A horses^{M-1} is a quadruped^P — Major premise
    All mammals^S breathe oxygen^{M-2} — Minor premise
    Therefore, some mammals^S are quadrupeds^P — Invalid (violates Rule I)

    All Romans^M were brave^P — Major premise
    Julius Caesar^S was a Roman^M — Minor premise
    Therefore, Julius Caesar^S was brave^P — Valid

    All horses^M are fast^P — Major premise
    Secretariat is a horse^M — Minor premise
    Therefore, some horses^M are fast^P — Invalid (violates Rule II)

    All food^{M-1} should be eaten^P — Major premise
    This logic problem^S is food for thought^{M-2} — Minor premise
    Therefore, this logic problem^S should be eaten^P — Invalid (violates Rule I)

23. Syllogisms given in answer to this question should have three and only three distinguishable terms and should not have the middle term in the conclusion.
24. T
    T
    F (In fact, it contains more than it should.)
    T
    F (Just the opposite is true.)
    T
    F (It occurs when the middle term appears in the conclusion.)
    T

_____ **Review Exercises for Day 4**

25. Reasoning is the act by which the mind acquires new knowledge by means of what it already knows.
26. First, we perceive the first premise as being true. Second, we perceive that the second premise is also true. The third step is an act of deductive inference. This third step takes place when we realize that, given the truth of the two premises, the conclusion must also be true.
27. A syllogism is a group of propositions in orderly sequence, one of which (the consequent) is said to be necessarily inferred from the others (the antecedent).
28. If the antecedent is true, the consequent must also be true.
29. If the syllogism is valid and the consequent is false, then the antecedent (i.e., one or both of the two premises) must be false.
30. In a valid syllogism with a true consequent, the antecedent is not necessarily true.
31. Two terms that are identical with a third term are identical to each other.
32. Two terms, one of which is identical with a third term and the other of which is nonidentical with that third term, are nonidentical to each other.
33. What is affirmed universally of a certain term is affirmed of every term that comes under that term.
34. What is denied universally of a certain term is denied of every term that comes under that term.

CHAPTER 12

_____ Exercises for Day 1

1. Quantitative rules for the validity of syllogisms.
2. Terminological Rules:
   I. There must be three and only three terms.
   II. The middle term must not occur in the conclusion.
   Quantitative Rules:
   III. If a term is not distributed in the premises, then it must not be distributed in the conclusion.
   IV. The middle term must be distributed at least once.
   Qualitative Rules:
   V. No conclusion can follow from two negative premises.
   VI. If the two premises are affirmative, the conclusion must also be affirmative.
   VII. If either premise is negative, the conclusion must be negative.
3. All seven.
4. Rules III and IV.
5. Because they have to do with the quantity of a statement in a syllogism.
6. With whether a statement is universal or particular.
7. The major, minor and middle terms.
8. The major term is the predicate of the conclusion; the minor term is the subject of the conclusion; the middle term is the term that appears in both of the premises, but not in the conclusion.
9. The premise which contains the major term.
10. The premise which contains the minor term.
11. If a term is distributed in the conclusion, then it must be distributed in the premises.
12. Saying more in the conclusion than is justified by the premises.
13. Distribution is the status of a term in regard to extension.
14. Extension has to do with how much a term refers to.
15. We mean that it has full extension; it extends to all members of the class to which the term refers.
16. We mean that it does not have full extension; that it does not extend to all the members of the class to which the term refers.
17. By writing a lowercase *d* next to the letter than indicates which term it is (i.e., *S*, *P*, or *M*)
18. By writing a *u* next to the letter that indicates which term it is.

_____ Exercises for Day 2

19.
DIAGRAM OF THE DISTRIBUTION OF
TERMS IN A, I, E, AND O STATEMENTS

Type of sentence	Subject-Term	Predicate-Term	Categorical Statements
A	Distributed	Undistributed	All S is P
I	Undistributed	Undistributed	Some S is P
E	Distributed	Distributed	No S is P
O	Undistributed	Distributed	Some S is not P

20. All men^{Md} are mortal^{Pu}
   Socrates^{Sd} is a man^{Mu}
   Therefore, Socrates^{Sd} is mortal^{Pu}

   All boys^{Md} are human^{Pu}
   Nathaniel^{Sd} is a boy^{Mu}
   Therefore, Nathaniel^{Sd} is human^{Pu}

   All kings^{Md} are good^{Pu}
   Hussein^{Sd} is a king^{Mu}
   Therefore, Hussein^{Sd} is good^{Pu}

   No truth^{Md} is simple^{Pd}
   Christianity^{Sd} is the truth^{Mu}
   Therefore, Christianity^{Sd} is not simple^{Pd}

No boys^{Md} are rude^{Pd}
Jeff^{Sd} is a boy^{Mu}
Therefore, Jeff^{Sd} is not rude^{Pd}

All cars^{Md} are fast^{Pu}
A Corvette^{Sd} is a car^{Mu}
Therefore, a Corvette^{Sd} is fast^{Pu}

All girls^{Md} are pretty^{Pu}
Suzy^{Sd} is a girl^{Mu}
Therefore, Suzy^{Sd} is pretty^{Pu}

All Romans^{Md} are brave^{Pu}
Caesar^{Sd} is a Roman^{Mu}
Therefore, Caesar^{Sd} is brave^{Pu}

All generals^{Md} are great^{Pu}
Hannibal^{Sd} is a general^{Mu}
Therefore, Hannibal^{Sd} is great^{Pu}

No wars^{Md} are fun^{Pd}
World War II^{Sd} was a war^{Mu}
Therefore, World War II^{Sd} was no fun^{Pd}

21. The Fallacy of Illicit Process.
22. By the commission of the Fallacy of Illicit Major and the Fallacy of Illicit Minor.
23. The Fallacy of Illicit Major is committed when the major term is distributed in the conclusion but not in the premises.
24. The Fallacy of Illicit Minor is committed when the minor term is distributed in the conclusion but not in the premises.
25.

All boys^{Md} are human^{Pu}
No girls^{Sd} are boys^{Md}
Therefore, no girls^{Sd} are human^{Pd}
■ Rule I ■ Rule II
Rule III: ■ IMn (■ IMj)

All victories^{Md} are glorious^{Pu}
No defeat^{Sd} is a victory^{Md}
Therefore, no defeat^{Sd} is glorious^{Pd}
■ Rule I ■ Rule II
Rule III: ■ IMn (■ IMj)

All men^{Md} are animals^{Pu}
All men^{Md} are mortal^{Su}
Therefore, all mortals^{Sd} are animals^{Pu}
■ Rule I ■ Rule II
Rule III: (■ IMn ■ IMj)

No boys^{Md} are cowards^{Pd}
All Latin students^{Sd} are boys^{Mu}
Therefore, no Latin students^{Sd} are cowards^{Pd}
■ Rule I ■ Rule II
Rule III: ■ IMn ■ IMj   (Valid)

All cars^{M-1d} are fast^{Pu}
My car^{M-2d} is a Corvette^{Su}
Therefore, my car^{Md} is fast^{Pu}
■ Rule I (■ Rule II)
Rule III: ■ IMn ■ IMj

All girls^{Pd} eat cookies^{M-1u}
All Girl Scouts^{Sd} sell cookies^{M-2u}
Therefore, all girls^{Sd} are Girl Scouts^{Pu}
(■ Rule I) ■ Rule II
Rule III: ■ IMn ■ IMj

All towns^{M-1d} are safe^{Pu}
Jerusalem^{Sd} has high walls^{M-2u}
Therefore, Jerusalem^{Sd} is safe^{Pu}
(■ Rule I) ■ Rule II
Rule III: ■ IMn ■ IMj

All Gorgons^{Md} have snaky hair^{Pu}
All Gorgons^{Md} are sisters^{Su}
Therefore, all sisters^{Sd} have snaky hair^{Pu}
■ Rule I ■ Rule II
Rule III: (■ IMn ■ IMj)

All Southerners^{Md} eat grits^{Pu}
No Yankee^{Sd} is a Southerner^{Md}
Therefore, no Yankee^{Sd} eats grits^{Pd}
■ Rule I ■ Rule II
Rule III: ■ IMn (■ IMj)

All Romans^{Md} are brave^{Pu}
No Gaul^{Sd} is a Roman^{Md}
Therefore, no Gaul^{Sd} is brave^{Pd}
■ Rule I ■ Rule II
Rule III: ■ IMn (■ IMj)

All generals^{Md} are great^{Pu}
All generals^{Md} are brave men^{Su}
Therefore, all brave men^{Sd} are great^{Pu}
■ Rule I ■ Rule II
Rule III: (■ IMn ■ IMj)

All wars^{Md} are cruel^{Pu}
No sports games^{Sd} are wars^{Md}
Therefore, no sports games^{Sd} are cruel^{Pd}
■ Rule I ■ Rule II
Rule III: ■ IMn (■ IMj)

_____ **Exercises for Day 3**

26. The middle term must be distributed at least once.
27. The Fallacy of Undistributed Middle.
28. Since the middle term is not distributed in either premise, it cannot serve to connect the minor and major terms, as is necessary in order to come to a conclusion.

29. All Gorgons^{Pd} have snaky hair^{Mu}
Medusa^{Sd} has snaky hair^{Mu}
Therefore, Medusa^{Sd} is a Gorgon^{Pu}
■ Rule I ■ Rule II
Rule III: ■ IMn ■ IMj
Rule IV: ⬤ FUM

All towns^{Md} are safe^{Pu}
Jerusalem^{Sd} is a town^{Mu}
Therefore, Jerusalem^{Sd} is safe^{Pu}
■ Rule I ■ Rule II
Rule III: ■ IMn ■ IMj
Rule IV: ■ FUM   (Valid)

No defeat^{Pd} is glorious^{Md}
All victories^{Sd} are glorious^{Mu}
Therefore, no victory^{Sd} is a defeat^{Pd}
■ Rule I ■ Rule II
Rule III: ■ IMn ■ IMj
Rule IV: ■ FUM   (Valid)

All queens^{Pd} are good^{Mu}
All kings^{Sd} are good^{Mu}
Therefore, all kings^{Sd} are queens^{Pu}
■ Rule I ■ Rule II
Rule III: ■ IMn ■ IMj
Rule IV: ⬤ FUM

All princes^{Md} are handsome^{Pu}
Some toads^{Su} are not princes^{Md}
Therefore, some toads^{Su} are not handsome^{Pd}
■ Rule I ■ Rule II
Rule III: ■ IMn ⬤ IMj
Rule IV: ■ FUM

All opera stars^{Md} sing songs^{Pu}
No sirens^{Sd} are opera stars^{Md}
Therefore, no sirens^{Sd} sing songs^{Pd}
■ Rule I ■ Rule II
Rule III: ■ IMn ⬤ IMj
Rule IV: ■ FUM

All heroes^{Md} are patriots^{Pu}
Charles Lindbergh^{Sd} is a hero^{Mu}
Therefore, Charles Lindbergh^{Sd} is a patriot^{Pu}
■ Rule I ■ Rule II
Rule III: ■ IMn ■ IMj
Rule IV: ■ FUM   (Valid)

Some dull things^{Mu} are valuable^{Pu}
All homework^{Sd} is dull^{Mu}
Therefore, some homework^{Su} is valuable^{Pu}
■ Rule I ■ Rule II
Rule III: ■ IMn ■ IMj
Rule IV: ⬤ FUM

Some merry men^{Mu} live in Sherwood Forest^{Pu}
All archers^{Sd} are merry men^{Mu}
Therefore, some archers^{Su} live in Sherwood^{Pu}
■ Rule I ■ Rule II
Rule III: ■ IMn ■ IMj
Rule IV: ⬤ FUM

Some great generals^{Mu} defeated Rome^{Pu}
Hannibal^{Sd} was a great general^{Mu}
Therefore, Hannibal^{Sd} defeated Rome^{Pu}
■ Rule I ■ Rule II
Rule III: ■ IMn ■ IMj
Rule IV: ⬤ FUM

All merry men^{Pd} are archers^{Mu}
Robin Hood^{Sd} is an archer^{Mu}
Therefore, Robin Hood^{Sd} is a merry man^{Pu}
■ Rule I ■ Rule II
Rule III: ■ IMn ■ IMj
Rule IV: ⬤ FUM

All toads^{Md} are ugly^{Pu}
No princes^{Sd} are toads^{Md}
Therefore, no princes^{Sd} are ugly^{Pd}
■ Rule I ■ Rule II
Rule III: ■ IMn ⬤ IMj
Rule IV: ■ FUM

_____ **Exercises for Day 4**

30. Some green men^{Mu} are leprechauns^{Pu}
Some green men^{Mu} are Martians^{Su}
Therefore, some Martians^{Su} are leprechauns^{Pu}
■ Rule I ■ Rule II
Rule III: ■ IMn ■ IMj
Rule IV: ⬤ FUM

All towns$^{\text{M-1d}}$ are safe^{Pu}
Jerusalem$^{\text{M-2d}}$ is a holy city^{Su}
Therefore, some holy cities^{Su} are safe^{Pu}
⬤ Rule I ■ Rule II
Rule III: ■ IMn ■ IMj
Rule IV: ■ FUM

All leopards^{Pd} are felines^{Mu}
All lions^{Sd} are felines^{Mu}
Therefore, some lions^{Su} are leopards^{Pu}
■ Rule I ■ Rule II
Rule III: ■ IMn ■ IMj
Rule IV: ■ FUM

All oaks^{Md} are trees^{Pu}
No maples^{Sd} are oaks^{Md}
Therefore, no maples^{Sd} are trees^{Pd}
■ Rule I ■ Rule II
Rule III: ■ IMn ■ IMj
Rule IV: ■ FUM

No irrational thing^{Md} is a man^{Pd}
All beasts^{Sd} are irrational^{Mu}
Therefore, no beast^{Sd} is a man^{Pd}
■ Rule I ■ Rule II
Rule III: ■ IMn ■ IMj (Valid)
Rule IV: ■ FUM

Some rodents^{Mu} are a threat^{Pu}
All mice^{Sd} are rodents^{Mu}
Therefore, no mice^{Sd} are a threat^{Pd}
■ Rule I ■ Rule II
Rule III: ■ IMn ■ IMj
Rule IV: ■ FUM

All kings^{Md} are good^{Pu}
All kings^{Md} are rich^{Su}
Therefore, all rich people^{Sd} are good^{Pu}
■ Rule I ■ Rule II
Rule III: ■ IMn ■ IMj
Rule IV: ■ FUM

All ducks^{Pd} are birds^{Mu}
All birds^{Md} have feathers^{Su}
Therefore some birds^{Mu} are not ducks^{Pd}
■ Rule I ■ Rule II
Rule III: ■ IMn ■ IMj
Rule IV: ■ FUM

31. (Check these answers to make sure they comply with Rules I-IV.)
32. T
    T
    F (The Fallacy of Illicit Process is committed when Rule III, not Rule IV, is violated.)
    T
    T
    F (The Fallacy of Undistributed Middle is committed when the minor term is not distributed at least once. The middle term should never appear in the conclusion)

CHAPTER 13

_____ Exercises for Day 1

1. Qualitative rules for the validity of syllogisms.
2. Terminological Rules:
   I.   There must be three and only three terms.
   II. The middle term must not occur in the conclusion.
   Quantitative Rules:
   III. If a term is not distributed in the premises, then it must not be distributed in the conclusion.
   IV. The middle term must be distributed at least once.
   Qualitative Rules:
   V.   No conclusion can follow from two negative premises.
   VI. If the two premises are affirmative, the conclusion must also be affirmative.
   VII. If either premise is negative, the conclusion must be negative.
3. All seven.
4. The last three.
5. Because they have to do with the *quality* of the statements in a syllogism.
6. It has to do with whether it is affirmative or negative.
7. The major, minor, and middle terms.
8. The major term is the predicate of the conclusion; the minor term is the subject of the conclusion; the middle term is the term that is present in both of the premises, but not in the conclusion.
9. The premise that contains the minor term.
10. The premise that contains the major term.

11.   DIAGRAM OF THE DISTRIBUTION OF
      TERMS IN A, I, E, AND O STATEMENTS

Type of sentence	Subject-Term	Predicate-Term	Categorical Statements
A	Distributed	Undistributed	All S is P
I	Undistributed	Undistributed	Some S is P
E	Distributed	Distributed	No S is P
O	Undistributed	Distributed	Some S is not P

——————— **Exercises for Day 2**

12. No conclusion can follow from two negative premises.
13. It prevents us from saying more in the conclusion than is in the premises.
14. The Fallacy of Exclusive Premises.
15.

No saints^Pd are villains^Md
Some robbers^Su are not villains^Md
Therefore, some robbers^Su are saints^Pu
- Rule I - Rule II
- Rule III - Rule IV - (Rule V)

Some vegetables^Mu are not sweet^Pd
No vegetable^Md is a fruit^Sd
Therefore some fruits^Su are not sweet^Pd
- Rule I - Rule II
- Rule III - Rule IV - (Rule V)

All floods^Md are devastating^Pu
No drought^Sd is a flood^Md
Therefore, no drought^Sd is devastating^Pd
- (Rule III) - Rule IV - Rule V
- Rule I - Rule II

All symphonies^Md are beautiful^Pu
No opera^Sd is a symphony^Md
Therefore, no opera^Sd is beautiful^Pd
- Rule I - Rule II
- (Rule III) - Rule IV - Rule V

All Protestants^Pd believe in the Trinity^Mu
All Catholics^Sd believe in the Trinity^Mu
Therefore, some Catholics^Su are Protestant^Pu
- Rule I - Rule II
- Rule III - (Rule IV) - Rule V

No maples^Pd are pines^Md
No oaks^Sd are pines^Md
Therefore, no oaks^Sd are maples^Pd
- Rule I - Rule II
- Rule III - Rule IV - (Rule V)

No Greeks^Pd are Romans^Md
Some soldiers^Su are not Romans^Md
Therefore, some soldiers^Su are not Greeks^Pd
- Rule I - Rule II
- Rule III - Rule IV - (Rule V)

No man^Md is as wise as Solomon^Pd
Einstein^Sd is a man^Mu
Therefore, Einstein^Sd is not as wise as Solomon^Pd
- Rule I - Rule II
- Rule III - Rule IV - Rule V   (Valid)

No tornadoes^Md are pleasant^Pd
Some violent storms^Su are tornadoes^Mu
Therefore, no violent storms^Sd are pleasant^Pd
- Rule I - Rule II
- (Rule III) - Rule IV - Rule V

Some merry men^Mu are not in Sherwood Forest^Pd
No sheriff^Sd is a merry man^Md
Therefore, no sheriff^Sd is in Sherwood Forest^Pd
- Rule I - Rule II
- Rule III - Rule IV - (Rule V)

——————— **Exercises for Day 3**

16. If the two premises are affirmative, the conclusion must also be affirmative.
17. The Fallacy of Drawing a Negative Conclusion from Affirmative Premises.
18.

All mermaids^Md can swim^Pu
Some nymphs^Su are mermaids^Mu
Therefore, some nymphs^Su are not swimmers^Pd
- Rule I - Rule II
- (Rule III) - Rule IV - Rule V
- (Rule VI)

All teeth^Md are white^Pu
A molar^Sd is a tooth^Mu
Therefore, a molar^Sd is white^Pu
- Rule I - Rule II
- Rule III - Rule IV - Rule V
- Rule VI   (Valid)

All revolutions^Pd are bloody^Mu
No election^Sd is bloody^Md
Therefore, no election^Sd is a revolution^Pd
- Rule I - Rule II
- Rule III - Rule IV - Rule V
- Rule VI   (Valid)

All jesters^Pd are clowns^Mu
All clowns^Md are funny^Su
Therefore, some funny people^Su are not jesters^Pd
- Rule I - Rule II
- Rule III - Rule IV - Rule V
- (Rule VI)

All archers^{Pd} are foresters^{Mu}
All foresters^{Md} are merry men^{Su}
Therefore, some merry men^{Su} aren't archers^{Pd}
■ Rule I ■ Rule II
■ Rule III ■ Rule IV ■ Rule V
(Rule VI)

No boys^{Md} are rude^{Pd}
No girls^{Sd} are boys^{Md}
Therefore, no girls^{Sd} are rude^{Pd}
■ Rule I ■ Rule II
■ Rule III ■ Rule IV (■ Rule V)
■ Rule VI

All queens^{Md} are regal^{Pu}
Elizabeth^{Sd} is a queen^{Mu}
Therefore, Elizabeth^{Sd} is regal^{Pu}
■ Rule I ■ Rule II
■ Rule III ■ Rule IV ■ Rule V
■ Rule VI   (Valid)

All oaks^{Pd} are trees^{Mu}
All trees^{Md} are alive^{Su}
Therefore, some living things^{Su} are not oaks^{Pd}
■ Rule I ■ Rule II
■ Rule III ■ Rule IV ■ Rule V
(■ Rule VI)

All military leaders^{Pd} are male^{Mu}
Joan of Arc^{Sd} is not a male^{Md}
Therefore, Joan of Arc^{Sd} is not a military leader^{Pd}
■ Rule I ■ Rule II
■ Rule III ■ Rule IV ■ Rule V
■ Rule VI   (Valid)

All Romans^{Md} are brave^{Pu}
Some Gauls^{Su} are not Romans^{Md}
Therefore, some Gauls^{Su} are not brave^{Pd}
■ Rule I ■ Rule II
(■ Rule III) ■ Rule IV ■ Rule V
■ Rule VI

All moons^{Md} are spherical^{Pu}
All moons^{Md} revolve^{Su}
Therefore, all things that revolve^{Sd} are spherical^{Pu}
■ Rule I ■ Rule II
(■ Rule III) ■ Rule IV ■ Rule V
■ Rule VI

All beagles^{Pd} are dogs^{Mu}
All dogs^{Md} are loyal^{Su}
Therefore, some loyal things^{Su} aren't beagles^{Pd}
■ Rule I ■ Rule II
■ Rule III ■ Rule IV ■ Rule V
(■ Rule VI)

Exercises for Day 4

19. Some fairies^{Pu} are not leprechauns^{Md}
All leprechauns^{Md} are green men^{Su}
Therefore, some green men^{Su} are fairies^{Pu}
■ Rule I ■ Rule II
■ Rule III ■ Rule IV ■ Rule V
■ Rule VI (■ Rule VII)

No revolutions^{Pd} are bloody^{Md}
All elections^{Sd} are bloody^{Mu}
Therefore, no election^{Sd} is a revolution^{Pd}
■ Rule I ■ Rule II
■ Rule III ■ Rule IV ■ Rule V
■ Rule VI ■ Rule VII   (Valid)

No noble thing^{Pd} is revered^{Md}
All heroes^{Sd} are revered^{Mu}
Therefore, no hero^{Sd} is a noble thing^{Pd}
■ Rule I ■ Rule II
■ Rule III ■ Rule IV ■ Rule V
■ Rule VI ■ Rule VII   (Valid)

All teeth^{Md} are white^{Pu}
All teeth^{Md} are molars^{Su}
Therefore, some molars^{Su} are white^{Pu}
■ Rule I ■ Rule II
■ Rule III ■ Rule IV ■ Rule V
■ Rule VI ■ Rule VII   (Valid)

No oaks^{Md} are pines^{Pd}
Some trees^{Su} are oaks^{Mu}
Therefore, some trees^{Su} are pines^{Pu}
■ Rule I ■ Rule II
■ Rule III ■ Rule IV ■ Rule V
■ Rule VI (■ Rule VII)

No hawks^{Md} are warblers^{Pd}
Some birds^{Su} are hawks^{Mu}
Therefore, some birds^{Su} are warblers^{Pu}
■ Rule I ■ Rule II
■ Rule III ■ Rule IV ■ Rule V
■ Rule VI (■ Rule VII)

20. (Make sure that syllogisms given in answer to this question comply with each of the seven rules.)
21. F (In this case it would violate Rule I.)
F (It could have one negative premise, in which case the conclusion must be negative.)
T
T
T
F (The only case in which it must be universal is if it is the minor term in the premise when the minor term in the conclusion is universal.)

CHAPTER 14

_____ Exercises for Day 1

1. | Mental Act | Verbal Expression |
    |---|---|
    | ■ Simple Apprehension | ■ Term |
    | ■ Judgment | ■ Proposition |
    | ■ Deductive Inference | ■ Syllogism |

2. F (Only the act of the mind grasping the essence or nature of a thing is the act itself.)
    T
    F (The chair exists outside the mind and the sense perception inside the mind.)
    T
    T
    T
    F (The idea of a chair in your mind need not be accompanied by the sense perception or the mental image.)
    F (While the simple apprehension is an act by which the mind grasps the concept or general meaning of an object, it does not affirm or deny anything about it. If it did, it would be a judgment, not a simple apprehension.)
    T
    F (Only sense perceptions and mental images can have shape and color.)
    T
    F (Mental images of the same essence can differ.)
    T
    T

3. F (they are _comprehension_ and _extension_, not _concept_ and _extension_.)
    T
    F (Aristotle said this, not Porphry.)
    T (The student might say this is false, thinking that it is _substance_, rather than being _sentient_, that determines whether it is something rather than nothing; however, if something is sentient, then it must be a substance [there are not things that are sentient that are not substance] and therefore it must be something rather than nothing.)
    F (The concept _man_ has 5 notes.)
    T
    F (_Man_ has greater comprehension but less extension than _body_: there are fewer men who have ever lived, are living, and ever will live than there are things that have substance that ever were, are, or will be.)
    T
    T

_____ Exercises for Day 2

4. F (They are the properties of simple apprehension rather than term.)
    T
    F (It is an example of a univocal term.)
    T
    F (They have entirely different and unrelated meanings, even though they are spelled or pronounced exactly the same way.)
    F (Analogous terms are applied to different terms but have related meanings.)
    T
    F (_Window_ is an analogous term.)
    T
    F (Scientific terms are primarily univocal terms.)
    F (This is how terms are divided up according to their supposition.)
    F (Material supposition occurs when a term refers to something as it exists _verbally_.)
    F (See explanation of previous answer.)
    T
    T
    T

5.   T
      F (Because a judgment could also separate two concepts by denying.)
      F (Judgment is the second part of the study of logic; deductive inference is the third.)
      F (The subject and the predicate are united by the copula.)
      F (The subject of the sentence is *man.*)
      F (The subject is *man.*)
      T
      F (It is a *command*, not a *proposition.*)
      T
      T
      F (It can have one or more words.)

6.   All kings are good: *affirmative, universal*
      No truth is simple: *negative, universal*
      Some generals are great: *affirmative, particular*
      Some Gauls are not brave: *negative, particular*
      All Romans are brave: *affirmative, universal*
      Some wars are not cruel: *negative, particular*
      All Christians are brothers: *affirmative, universal*
      No wars are peaceful: *negative, universal*

      Some towns are well fortified: *affirmative, particular*
      All truth is God's truth: *affirmative, universal*
      Some towns are not fortified: *negative, particular*
      Some victories are not glorious: *negative, particular*
      No tribes are safe: *negative, universal*
      All leaders are slaughtered: *affirmative, universal*
      Some wars are fierce: *affirmative, particular*
      No kings are good: *negative, universal*

_____ **Exercises for Day 3**

7.   F (They must also differ with each other in quantity.)
      F
      T
      T
      F (But they can both be false.)
      T
      T
      F ("Just do it" is not a proposition at all.)
      T
      F (Contrary statements cannot both be true, but can both be false.)

8.   T
      F (The *quantity*, not the *quality*, is universal.)
      T
      F (They only differ in quantity.)
      T
      T
      T
      F (The statement "Just do it" isn't even a proposition.)
      T
      F (Subalternate statements can both be false.)

9.   T
      F
      T
      F
      F
      T
      F (The statement "Just do it" isn't even a proposition.)
      T
      F (Subalternate statements can both be false.)

10.   O
      C
      C
      CP
      CP
      C
      O
      C
      O
      CP
      CP
      O
      O
      CP

_____ **Exercises for Day 4**

11.   F (It is the act of the mind by which we derive one truth from other truths we already know.)
      T
      F (It contains *two* premises.)
      T
      T
      T
      F (It is in both premises, but not the conclusion.)
      T

12.   T
      T
      F (In fact, it contains more than it should.)
      T
      F (Just the opposite is true.)
      T
      F (It occurs when the middle term appears in the conclusion.)
      T.

13.   T
      T
      F (The Fallacy of Illicit Process is committed when Rule III is violated.)
      T
      T
      F (The middle term should never appear in the conclusion.)

14.   F (In this case, it would violate Rule I.)
      F (It could have one negative premise, in which case the conclusion must be negative.)
      T
      T
      T
      F (The only case in which it must be universal is if it is the minor term in the premise when the minor term in the conclusion is universal.)

QUIZZES & FINAL EXAM

Answer Key

TRADITIONAL LOGIC I
Introduction Quiz

Name _____ Date _____ Score _____

What is the definition of logic?
Logic is the science of right thinking.

What are the two main branches of logic?
1. formal or "minor" logic
2. material or "major" logic

Define the following terms:
1. Truth correspondence to reality
2. Validity: when the conclusion follows logically from the premises
3. Soundness: when all the premises are true and the argument is valid

True/False Questions:
1. T (F) The purpose of formal logic is to discover truth.
2. (T) F A statement can be true or false.
3. T (F) An argument can be true or false.
4. (T) F A sound argument must be valid.
5. T (F) A valid argument must be sound.

Fill in the following chart. List the three acts of the mind involved in logic and their corresponding verbal expressions:

Mental Acts	Verbal Expressions
Simple Apprehension	Term
Judgment	Proposition (or statement)
Deductive Inference	Syllogism

ANSWER KEY

TRADITIONAL LOGIC I
Chapter 1 Quiz

Name_____Date_____Score_____

What are the three things associated with simple apprehension?

1.   Sense Perception_____

2.   Mental Image_____

3.   Concept_____

Give a definition of *sense perception.*

the act of seeing or hearing or smelling or tasting or touching_____

_____

Give the definition of *mental image.*

the image of an object formed in the mind as a result of a sense perception of that object_____

_____

Give the definition of *simple apprehension.*

an act by which the mind grasps the concept or general meaning of an object without affirming or denying anything about it

_____

True/False Questions:

1.   T   (F)   Mental image is the simple apprehension itself.

2.   (T)   F   Sense perception is the act of seeing or hearing or smelling or tasting or touching.

3.   T   (F)   The idea of a chair in your mind must be accompanied by the sense perception of a chair or by the mental image of a chair.

4.   (T)   F   When we have a simple apprehension of a thing, we grasp the thing's essence.

5.   (T)   F   If we were to affirm or deny something about a concept, we would be going beyond simple apprehension to judgment.

Fill in the following chart listing the three acts of the mind involved in logic and their corresponding verbal expressions:

Mental Acts	Verbal Expressions
Simple Apprehension	Term
Judgment	Proposition (or statement)
Deductive Inference	Syllogism

TRADITIONAL LOGIC I
Chapter 2 Quiz

Name_____ Date_____ Score_____

Indicate the number of notes possessed by the following concepts (circle the correct number):

1. man   1   2   3   4   ⑤

2. chair   1   ②   3   4   5

3. rock   1   ②   3   4   5

4. dog   1   2   3   ④   5

5. angel   ①   2   3   4   5

6. oak tree   1   2   ③   4   5

What is the extension of the concept 'man'?

all the men there are, ever were, and ever will be

What is the extension of the concept 'animal'?

all the animals that there are, ever were, and ever will be

What is the comprehension of the concept 'grass'?

non-sentient, living material substance (3 notes)

What is the comprehension of the concept 'wall'?

non-living material substance (2 notes)

Underline the concept with the greatest extension:

1. man   <u>body</u>
2. <u>body</u>   animal
3. <u>substance</u>   man
4. animal   <u>substance</u>
5. man   <u>substance</u>
6. body   <u>substance</u>
7. <u>animal</u>   man

True/False Questions:

1. Ⓣ   F   If something is sentient, then it is something rather than nothing.

2. Ⓣ   F   The concept 'man' has greater comprehension than the concept 'body.'

3. Ⓣ   F   The concept 'man' has greater comprehension than the concept 'animal.'

4. T   Ⓕ   Porphyry once said that man is a "featherless biped."

ANSWER KEY

TRADITIONAL LOGIC I
Chapter 3 Quiz

Name_____·_____Date_____Score_____

What are the two properties of terms?

significance and supposition

Give a definition of *term*:

a word or group of words that verbally expresses a concept

What are the three ways terms can be divided according to signification?

1. Univocal terms
2. Equivocal terms
3. Analogus terms

What are univocal terms?

terms that have exactly the same meaning no matter when or how they are used

Give three univocal terms not used in the book:

1. computer
2. plywood
3. steering wheel

What are equivocal terms?

terms that, although spelled and pronounced exactly alike, have entirely different and unrelated meanings

Give three equivocal terms not used in the book:

1. pitch
2. project
3. pool

What are analogous terms?:

terms that are applied to different things, but have related meanings

Give three analogous terms not used in the book:

1. fortune
2. bright
3. air

What is material supposition?

The use of a term according to its verbal existence.

What is logical supposition?

The use of a term according to its mental or logical existence

What is real supposition?

The use of a term according to its real or actual existence.

True/False Questions:

1. T (F) The term 'photosynthesis' is an example of an equivocal term.

2. T (F) Equivocal terms have related meanings.

3. T (F) Many analogous terms are scientific terms.

4. T (F) Material supposition occurs when a term refers to something as it exists in the real world.

5. (T) F The three aspects of logic are simple apprehension, judgment, and deductive inference.

TRADITIONAL LOGIC I
Chapter 4 Quiz

Name_____Date_____ Score_____

What is the definition of *judgment*?

the act by which the intellect unites by affirming, or separates by denying

_____

What does a judgment unite (or separate)?

Judgment unites or separates two concepts.

_____

What is the definition of *proposition*?

a sentence or statement that expresses truth or falsity

_____

Give three examples of sentences that are propositions:

1. Boys are wild.
2. Snails love to take their time.
3. Politicians don't understand the public.

Give three examples of sentences that are *not* propositions:

1. Why haven't you made your bed.
2. You should go for it!
3. Who do you think you are?

What are the three elements of any proposition:

1. the subject-term
2. the predicate-term
3. the copula

Explain what the subject-term is:

the verbal expression of the subject of a judgment

_____

Explain what the predicate-term is:

the verbal expression of the predicate of a judgment

_____

Explain what the copula is:

the word in the proposition that connects or relates the subject to the predicate

_____

ANSWER KEY   TRADITIONAL LOGIC I
Chapter 5 Quiz

Name_____ Date_____ Score_____

Tell whether the following are A, I, E, or O statements, and indicate the quantity and quality of each:

All terrorists are hijackers.

Type of Statement: __A__
Quantity: __Universal__
Quality: __Affirmative__

Some letters contain anthrax.

Type of Statement: __I__
Quantity: __Particular__
Quality: __Affirmative__

No terrorists are hijackers.

Type of Statement: __E__
Quantity: __Universal__
Quality: __Negative__

All letters contain anthrax.

Type of Statement: __A__
Quantity: __Universal__
Quality: __Affirmative__

Some terrorists are not hijackers.

Type of Statement: __O__
Quantity: __Particular__
Quality: __Negative__

Some letters contain no anthrax.

Type of Statement: __O__
Quantity: __Particular__
Quality: __Negative__

Some terrorists are hijackers.

Type of Statement: __I__
Quantity: __Particular__
Quality: __Affirmative__

Afghanistan is an unpleasant place.

Type of Statement: __A__
Quantity: __Universal__
Quality: __Affirmative__

No letters contain anthrax.

Type of Statement: __E__
Quantity: __Universal__
Quality: __Negative__

Afghanistan is not an unpleasant place.

Type of Statement: __E__
Quantity: __Universal__
Quality: __Negative__

What are the four components of a proposition?

1. Quantifier
2. Subject Term
3. Predicate Term
4. Copula

Write a statement that is an affirmative universal statement:

All _____ is _____

Write a statement that is a negative universal statement:

No _____ is _____

Write a statement that is an affirmative particular statement:

Some _____ is _____

Write a statement that is a negative particular statement:

Some _____ is not _____

TRADITIONAL LOGIC I
Chapter 6–7 Quiz

Name _____ Date _____ Score _____

What are the two kinds of relationships statements can have to one another?

1. Opposition
2. Equivalence

What are the four ways A, I, E, and O statements can be related to one another in opposition?

1. Contradiction
2. Contrariety
3. Subcontrariety
4. Subalternation

Use the letters A, I, E, and O to indicate the statements in your answer

1. **Which two pairs of statements are contradictory?**
   A and O; and E and I
2. **Which types of statements are contrary?**
   A and E
3. **Which types of statements are subcontrary?**
   I and O
4. **Which types of statements are subalternate?**
   A and I; and E and O

Write two pairs of statements that are contradictory. Use all the possible combinations of types of statements that can be contradictory in your answer (i.e. use all the types of statements indicated in your answer to question three):

1. This should be an A statement   This should be an O statement
2. This should be an E statement   This should be an I statement

Write two statements that are contrary to one another:

This should be an A statement   This should be an E statement

Write two statements that are subcontrary to one another:

This should be an I statement   This should be an O statement

Write two pairs of statements that are subalternate. Use all the possible types of statements that can be subalternate (i.e. use all the types of statements indicated in your answer to question 6.):

1. This should be an A statement   This should be an I statement
2. This should be an E statement   This should be an O statement

Draw a Square of Opposition:

A   C O N T R A R I E S   E

All S is P   No S is P

CONTRADICTORIES

Some S is P   Some S is not P

I   S U B C O N T R A R I E S   O

TRADITIONAL LOGIC I
Chapter 8 Quiz

Name_____ Date_____ Score_____

Fill out the following diagram indicating distribution by d (distributed) or u (undistributed):

Type of Statement	Subject-term	Predicate-term
A	Distributed (d)	Undistributed (u)
I	Undistributed (u)	Undistributed (u)
E	Distributed (d)	Distributed (d)
O	Undistributed (u)	Distributed (d)

Diagram these statements:

All men are mortal.

No men are happy

Some men are happy.

Some men are not happy

TRADITIONAL LOGIC I
Chapter 9 Quiz

Name_____Date_____Score_____

What are the three ways in which statements can be converted into their logical equivalents?

1. Obversion
2. Conversion
3. Contraposition

Give the two-step method for obverting a statement:

1. Change the quality of the statement.
2. Negate the predicate.

Circle each of the four statements that can be obverted:

Ⓐ Ⓘ Ⓔ Ⓞ

Tell how to convert a statement:

Interchange the subject and the predicate.

Circle each of the four statements that can be converted:

A Ⓘ Ⓔ O

What is partial conversion?

Partial conversion is accomplished by interchanging the subject and predicate and changing the statement from universal to particular. It is the only way to "convert" an A statement.

Give the three-step method for contraposing a statement:

1. Obvert the statement.
2. Convert the statement.
3. Obvert the statement again.

Circle each of the four statements that can be contraposed:

Ⓐ I E Ⓞ

Obvert, convert, and contrapose the statements below wherever possible (partially convert wherever necessary):

All men are mortal.	Some men are happy

Obvert: No men are immortal.

Obvert: Some men are not non-happy (unhappy)

Convert: Some mortal things are men. (partial conversion)

Convert: Some happy things are men.

Contrapose: All immortal things are not men.

Contrapose: You cannot contrapose an I statement.

No men are gods.

Obvert: All men are not gods.

Convert: No gods are men.

Contrapose: You cannot contrapose an E statement.

Some men are not happy.

Obvert: Some men are not happy.

Convert: You cannot convert an O statement.

Contrapose: Some unhappy things are men.

ANSWER KEY   TRADITIONAL LOGIC I
Chapter 10 Quiz

Name_____ Date_____ Score_____

What is the definition of reasoning?

Reasoning is the act by which the mind acquires new knowledge by means of what it already knows.

What are the two kinds of reasoning?

1. Deductive reasoning
2. Inductive reasoning

What is the definition of deductive inference?

Deductive inference is the act by which the mind establishes a connection between the antecedent and the consequent.

What is the definition of syllogism?

A syllogism is a group of propositions in orderly sequence, one of which (the consequent) is said to be necessarily inferred from the others (the antecedent).

What is the Essential Law of Argumentation?

If the antecedent is true, then the consequent must also be true.

What are the three terms contained in a syllogism?

1. Major term
2. Minor term
3. Middle term

In a syllogism, which premise is the major premise?

The major premise is the premise that contains the major term.

In a syllogism, which premise is the minor premise?

The minor premise is the premise that contains the minor term.

What is the Dictum de Omni?

What is affirmed universally of a certain term is affirmed of every term that comes under that term.

What is the Dictum de Nullo?

What is denied universally of a certain term is denied of every term that comes under that term.

Indicate the major, minor, and middle terms in the following syllogisms as well as the major and minor premises:

All mammals breathe oxygen.
A horse is a mammal.
Therefore, a horse breathes oxygen.

Major Premise: ___All mammals breathe oxygen.___

Minor Premise: ___A horse is a mammal.___

P: ___things that breathe oxygen___

S: ___horse___

M: ___mammals___

All horses are fast.
Secretariat is a horse.
Therefore, Secretariat is fast.

Major Premise: ___All horses are fast.___

Minor Premise: ___Secretariat is a horse.___

P: ___fast things___

S: ___Secretariat___

M: ___horses___

All Americans are brave.
George Washington is an American.
Therefore, George Washington is brave.

Major Premise: ___All Americans are brave.___

Minor Premise: ___George Washington is an American.___

P: ___brave things___

S: ___George Washington___

M: ___Americans___

All wars are bloody.
The War of Roses was a war.
Therefore, the War of Roses was bloody.

Major Premise: ___All wars are bloody.___

Minor Premise: ___The War of Roses was a war.___

P: ___bloody things___

S: ___War of Roses___

M: ___wars___

True/False Questions:

1. T (F) A syllogism contains three premises and a conclusion.

2. T (F) The middle term is the term that does not appear in either premise.

3. (T) F In a valid argument, if the premises are true, the conclusion must be true.

4. (T) F The minor term is the subject of the conclusion and the major term is the predicate of the conclusion.

TRADITIONAL LOGIC I
Chapter 11 Quiz

Name_____Date_____Score_____

Indicate the two terminological rules for syllogisms:

1. There must be three and only three terms._____
2. The middle term must not occur in the conclusion._____

Fill in the blanks and indicate whether each of the following syllogisms is valid or invalid (by circling the proper response), and, if invalid, circle which rule it violates:

> All wildebeasts are mammals.
> All lions are felines.
> Therefore, all felines are mammals.

Major Premise: All wildebeasts are mammals.

Minor Premise: All lions are felines.

P: mammals

S: felines

M: no middle term

Valid or Invalid?: Invalid

If invalid, violates rule: ①   2

> All angels are created by God.
> Gabriel is an angel.
> Therefore, Gabriel is created by God.

Major Premise: All angels are created by God.

Minor Premise: Gabriel is an angel

P: things created by God

S: Gabriel

M: angels

Valid or Invalid?:   Valid

If invalid, violates rule: 1   2

> All mice eat cheese.
> Some computer parts are mice.
> Therefore, some computer parts eat cheese.

Major Premise: All mice eat cheese.

Minor Premise: Some computer parts are mice.

P: cheese

S: computer parts

M: mice

Valid or Invalid?:   Invalid

If invalid, violates rule: ①   2

ANSWER KEY

TRADITIONAL LOGIC I
Chapter 12 Quiz

Name_____ Date_____ Score_____

Indicate the major, minor, and middle terms, and the major and minor premises of each of the following syllogisms. Indicate whether each is valid or invalid, and if invalid, indicate which rule it violates:

All queens are good.
All kings are good.
Therefore, all kings are queens.

Major Premise: All queens are good.

Minor Premise: All kings are good.

P: queens

S: kings

M: good things

Valid or Invalid?: Invalid

If invalid, violates rule: 1   2   3   ④   5   6   7

All plants are living.
Some flowers are plants.
Therefore, some flowers are living.

Major Premise: All plants are living.

Minor Premise: Some flowers are plants.

P: living things

S: flowers

M: plants

Valid or Invalid?:   Valid

If invalid, violates rule: 1   2   3   4   5   6   7

No plants are animals.
All animals are living.
Therefore, no living things are plants.

Major Premise: No plants are animals.

Minor Premise: All animals are living.

P: plants

S: living things

M: animals

Valid or Invalid?:   invalid

If invalid, violates rule: 1   2   ③   4   5   6   7

True/False Questions:

1. ⓉF   Rule IV ensures that the major and minor term get connected.

2. ⓉF   A violation of Rule III results in a possibility of two different fallacies.

3. T Ⓕ   'Distribution' is the status of a term with regard to its comprehension.

TRADITIONAL LOGIC I
Chapter 13 Quiz

Name_____Date_____Score_____

Indicate the two quantitative rules for syllogisms:

1. If a term is distributed in the conclusion, then it must be distributed in the premises._____

2. _____
   The middle term must be distributed at least once._____

Indicate the three qualitative rules for syllogisms:

1. No conclusion can follow from two negative premises._____

2. _____
   If the two premises are affirmative, the conclusion must also be affirmative._____

3. If either premise is negative, the conclusion must be negative._____

Indicate the major, minor, and middle terms, and the major and minor premises of each of the following syllogisms. Indicate whether each is valid or invalid, and if invalid, indicate which rule it violates:

All men are mortal.
Socrates is a man.
Therefore, Socrates is mortal.

Major Premise:___All men are mortal.___
Minor Premise:___Socrates is a man.___
P:___mortal___
S:___Socrates___
M:___men___
Valid or Invalid?: Valid
If invalid, violates rule: 1   2   3   4   5   6   7

All victories are glorious.
No defeat is a victory.
Therefore, no defeat is glorious.

Major Premise:___All victories are glorious.___
Minor Premise:___No defeat is a victory.___
P:___glorious things___
S:___defeat___
M:___victory___
Valid or Invalid?:___Invalid___
If invalid, violates rule: 1   2   ③   4   5   6   7

No hawks are warblers.
Some birds are hawks.
Therefore, some birds are warblers.

Major Premise:___No hawks are warblers.___
Minor Premise:___Some birds are hawks.___
P:___warblers___
S:___birds___
M:___hawks___
Valid or Invalid?:___invalid___
If invalid, violates rule: 1   2   3   4   5   6   ⑦

All mermaids can swim.
Some nymphs are mermaids.
Therefore, some nymphs are not swimmers.

Major Premise:___All mermaids can swim___
Minor Premise:___Some nymphs are mermaids.___
P:___swimmers___
S:___nymphs___
M:___mermaids___
Valid or Invalid?:___Invalid___
If invalid, violates rule: 1   2   ③   4   5   6   ⑦

> All men are animals
> All men are mortal.
> Therefore, all mortals are animals.

Major Premise: _All men are animals_

Minor Premise: _All men are mortal._

P: _animals_

S: _mortals_

M: _men_

Valid or Invalid?: _Invalid_

If invalid, violates rule: 1   2   ③   4   5   6   7

> No maples are pines.
> No oaks are pines.
> Therefore, no oaks are maples.

Major Premise: _No maples are pines._

Minor Premise: _No oaks are pines._

P: _maples_

S: _oaks_

M: _pines_

Valid or Invalid?: _Invalid_

If invalid, violates rule: 1   2   3   4   ⑤   6   7

True/False Questions:

1. T Ⓕ Syllogisms that violate Rule IV are said to commit the Fallacy of Illicit Process.

2. T Ⓕ If the middle term is not distributed in either of the premises, then the syllogism is valid.

ANSWER KEY

TRADITIONAL LOGIC I
Final Exam

Name_____Date_____Score_____

Indicate the three parts of logic on the following chart:

Mental Acts:

Simple Apprehension

Judgment

Deductive Inference

Verbal Expression:

Term

Proposition

Syllogism

Write the Four Statements of logic:

A: All S is P

I: Some S is P

E: No S is P

O: Some S is not P

Give the definitions of quality and quantity as they relate to statements:

Quality: The quality of a proposition has to do with whether it is affirmative or negative.

Quantity: The quantity of a proposition has to do with whether it is universal or particular.

Give the quality and quantity of each of the four statements:

	Quality	Quantity
A	Affirmative	Universal
I	Affirmative	Particular
E	Negative	Universal
O	Negative	Particular

Draw the square of opposition, indicating the four relationships of opposition:

A   C O N T R A R I E S   E

All S is P   No S is P

Contradictories

Contradictories

Some S is P   Some S is not P

I   SUBC O N T R A R I E S   O

Diagram these statements:

All men are animals.

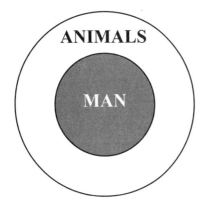

No men are reptiles

Some dogs are vicious things.

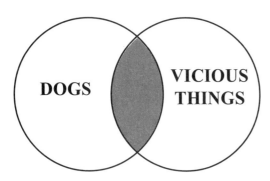

Some men are not blind

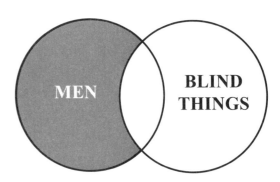

Complete the Diagram of Distribution:

	Subject-Term	Predicate-Term
A	distributed	undistributed
I	undistributed	undistributed
E	distributed	distributed
O	undistributed	distributed

Explain how to obvert a statement (give the steps):

Step #1: Change the quality of the statement

Step #2: Negate the predicate

Explain how to convert a statement (give the steps):

Interchange (or "switch") the subject and the predicate.

Explain how to contrapose a statement (give the steps):

Step #1: Obvert the statement

Step #2: Convert the statement

Step #3: Obvert the statement again

Identify and define the three terms in a syllogism:

Name of Term	Definition of Term
Minor Term	The term that is the subject of the conclusion
Major Term	The term that is the predicate of the conclusion
Middle Term	The term that appears in both premises but not the conclusion

Define the following terms:

major premise: The premise that contains the major term

minor premise: The premise that contains the minor term

Give the seven rules for validity:

1. There must be three and only three terms.

2. The middle term must not occur in the conclusion.

3. If a term is distributed in the conclusion, then it must be distributed in the premises.

4. The middle term must be distributed at least once.

5. No conclusion can follow from two negative premises.

6. If the two premises are affirmative, the conclusion must also be affirmative.

7. If either premise is negative, the conclusion must also be negative.